AMAZING SPACE

THE INTERNATIONAL SPACE STATION

BY LORI DITTMER

CREATIVE EDUCATION • CREATIVE PAPERBACKS

Published by Creative Education
and Creative Paperbacks
P.O. Box 227, Mankato, Minnesota 56002
Creative Education and Creative Paperbacks
are imprints of The Creative Company
www.thecreativecompany.us

Design by The Design Lab
Art direction by Graham Morgan
Edited by Ana Brauer

Photographs by NASA/Unknown, cover, 1, 2, 7, 9, 10, 17, 20, 21, 22–23; Wikimedia Commons/NASA, 5, 6, 13, 18, NASA/Bill Ingalls, 14, Outstandy, 8, Roscosmos, 16

Library of Congress Cataloging-in-Publication Data
Names: Dittmer, Lori, author.
Title: The International Space Station / by Lori Dittmer.
Other titles: Amazing space (Creative Education, Inc. (Mankato, Minn.))
Description: Mankato, Minnesota : Creative Education and Creative Paperbacks, [2025] | Series: Amazing space | Includes bibliographical references and index. | Audience: Ages 6–9 | Audience: Grades 2–3 | Summary: "Learn about the orbital research laboratory called the International Space Station (ISS). This astronomy title for elementary-aged kids includes captions, on-page definitions, a space science feature, additional STEM resources, and an index"— Provided by publisher.
Identifiers: LCCN 2024018579 (print) | LCCN 2024018580 (ebook) | ISBN 9798889892366 (library binding) | ISBN 9781682776025 (paperback) | ISBN 9798889893479 (ebook)
Subjects: LCSH: International Space Station—Juvenile literature.
Classification: LCC TL797.15 .D58 2025 (print) | LCC TL797.15 (ebook) | DDC 629.44/2—dc23/eng/20240508
LC record available at https://lccn.loc.gov/2024018579
LC ebook record available at https://lccn.loc.gov/2024018580

Table of Contents

Building the station took more than 10 years and 40 trips from Earth.

The International Space Station (ISS) is a laboratory in space. Groups from around the world worked together to build it. Scientists take turns living there. They do research and tests.

laboratory a place with special equipment for doing science experiments

The station has an observation deck that gives crew members a view of Earth.

The ISS is just 250 miles (402 km) above Earth. A spacecraft can reach it in about four hours. The station orbits Earth 16 times each day. It is close enough for us to see. We do not need a telescope.

orbit to travel in a path around an object in space

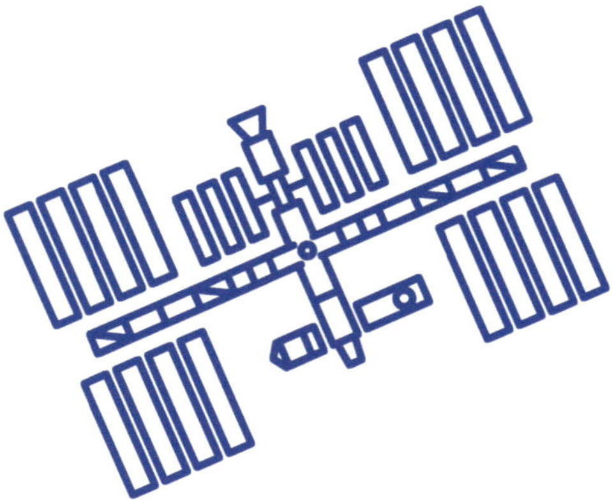

The ISS spans the length of a football field. Pieces of the station are shaped like canisters, spheres, triangles, and flat panels. Several spaceships can connect to the ISS at one time.

The best time to see the lights of the ISS is right before sunrise or after sunset.

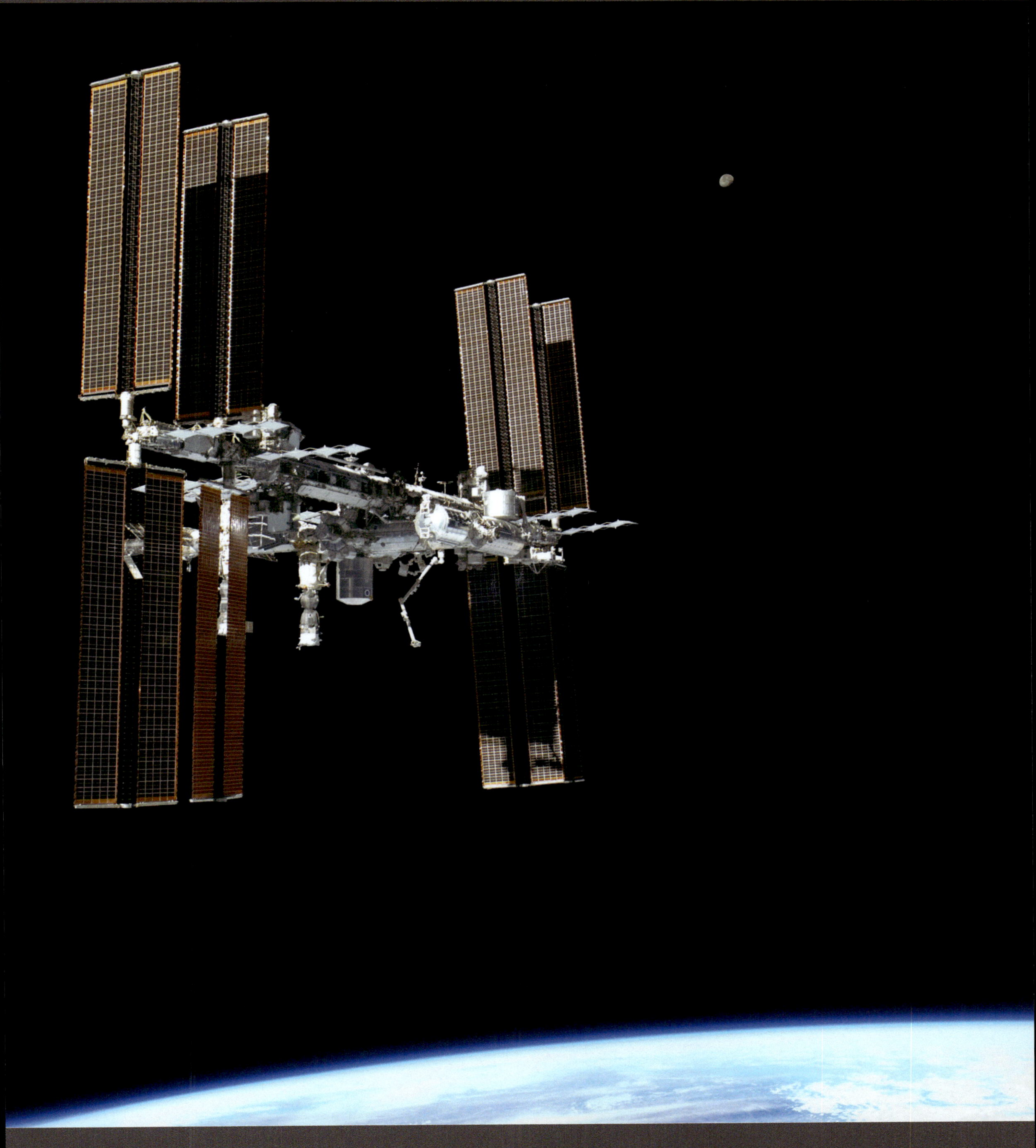

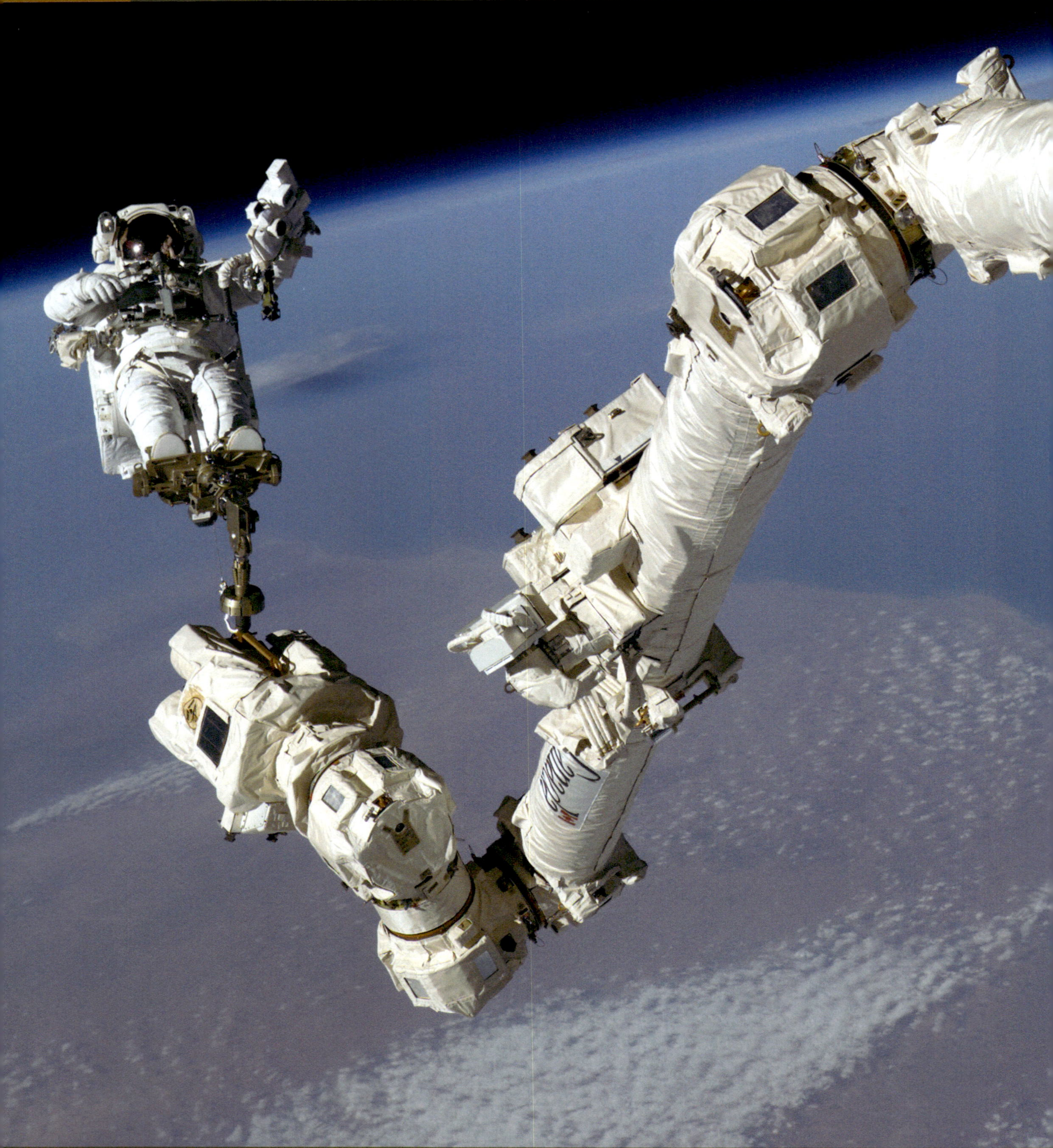

A long robotic arm helps with missions outside of the station. Huge solar panels absorb energy from the Sun. Solar energy is turned into electricity. This powers the station.

Crew members wear spacesuits and do spacewalks to work outside the ISS.

Crew members spend a lot of time doing research. They also make repairs inside and outside of the space station. To keep their bodies healthy, they eat meals stored in the galley. Each meal comes from a packet for one person. Nobody needs to wash dishes!

The ISS has two bathrooms, a gym, and seven sleeping pods.

CLOSING HATCH

The crew live and work within 16 modules of the ISS.

To build the ISS, rockets carried modules into space one at a time. The first one was launched in 1998. Astronauts put the pieces together. In 2000, a crew began living there. Since then, a crew of 3 to 13 people has lived on the station.

module one piece of a set that can be connected to build something

Five space agencies from around the world have worked on the station. This shows that great things can happen when people from different places work together. More than 270 astronauts from 21 countries have visited the ISS.

The agencies are from Canada, Japan, Russia, Europe, and the United States.

ССИЯ
МИСУРКИН
A. MISURKIN

ZERO G
OPENING HATCH
WARNING

Crew members sleep in sleeping bags that are strapped to the wall to keep them from floating around.

The gravity on the ISS is different than on Earth. This makes the station a great place to do research. Living in space makes muscles weak. People aboard the ISS exercise about two hours every day.

gravity the force that pulls everything to the ground

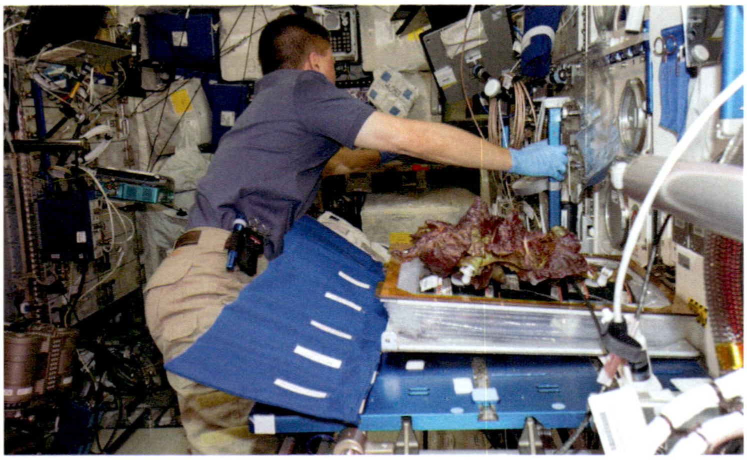

A crop of lettuce grown on the ISS.

Scientists have learned a lot from life on the ISS. This information will help them plan for the future. Someday, humans might live on Mars. Maybe they will go even deeper in space!

NASA plans to retire the ISS by 2030. A new station will take its place.

Spotlight: Research on the ISS

ISS crews have done thousands of science experiments. They hope to improve life on Earth and in space. They have found new ways to make medicines. They study new ways to treat diseases like cancer. They are working on new ways to make water safe to drink. They have grown plants in the space station. Crew members have studied themselves, too. Some have stayed on board for more than 300 days. They want to know how life in space affects the human body.

3
4

Read More

Finan, Catherine C. *The International Space Station.* Minneapolis: Bearport Publishing, 2022.

Markovics, Joyce L. *The International Space Station.* Norwood House Press, 2023.

Rector, Rebecca Kraft. *The International Space Station.* New York: Children's Press, 2022

Websites

Kiddle: International Space Station Facts for Kids
https://kids.kiddle.co/International_Space_Station
Read more about the ISS.

Spot the Station
spotthestation.nasa.gov
Find the location of the International Space Station and track its path..

Index